The Complete Poetical Works of Gerard A. Geiger

by

Gerard Geiger

Writers Club Press
San Jose New York Lincoln Shanghai

The Complete Poetical Works of Gerard A. Geiger

Copyright © 2000 by Gerard A. Geiger

This book may not be reproduced or distributed, in whole or in part, in print or by any other means without the written permission of the author.

ISBN: 0-595-09187-3

Published by Writers Club Press, an imprint of iUniverse.com, Inc.

For information address:
iUniverse.com, Inc.
620 North 48th Street
Suite 201
Lincoln, NE 68504-3467
www.iuniverse.com

URL: http://www.writersclub.com

Contents

When I go Sailing 1

Trees 2

The Universe 3

My Vessel 4

The Inevitable 5

Wandering 6

Earthlings 7

Whenever 8

Nature for the Civilized 10

King 11

Victory 12

A Prayer 14

Analysis of a Daydreamer 16

The Purposeless Man 17

Nightlife 18

Changes 20

Of Revelry and Reveille 21

Why?	22
The Fisherman	24
Termination	26
The Human Real	27
Rationalizing the Irrational	31
Thanksgiving 76	35
Honour	38
Indulgence	40
Crosswalk	41
The Relationship	43
On Living	45
On Security	47
Apathy	49
Reinforcement	51
On Love	52
Pleasant Forces	54
The Gifts	56
A Moment of Time	58
Commencement	60
Serendipity	61
Snowflake	63

My Woman	65
Tradition	67
Pauly the Penguin	68
Comfort	69
Santa's Gift	71
The Pursuit of Happiness	75
Bison (Ode to the American Buffalo)	76
Stolen Time	78
What was it?	80
Cindy	82
The Source	83
Aching Back	85
Christmas Remembered	86
Virus	89
Chameleon	91
Cut and Run	92
Ecstasy	94
"Mystery"	96
Whisper	98
The Challenge	100
Our Love: Young and New	102

Sentinel	105
The River	107
Tell me (what you need)	109
Dreams and Sand Castles	113
At Time's End	117
The Diary	121
The Devil You Now See	125
Reflections	129

Introduction

My first four poems were written in 1964/1965. I turned 11 years old in December 1964 and was in the sixth grade. I've become a lot older since then, but I doubt I've become more intelligent.

I've arranged these poems, chronologically, so that in some small measure the Reader can encounter them in the order they were written in my life. For those of you who like to jump ahead, feel free to do so.

Hope you enjoy…

                                                          Gerard   January 2000

The Complete Poetical Works of Gerard A. Geiger

The Complete Poetical Works—June 23, 1998 (written from 1964 to 1998) includes those works previously copyrighted under the titles *Santa's Gift*, *Ramblings*, and *Whispers*.

When I go Sailing

When I go sailing on my pond,
I have a feeling that I am far beyond,
Beyond the shores of the western sea,
Where many a man would wish he could be.

And when my vessel begins to float,
I stand at the stern of my little boat.
And I could sail forevermore
Towards my make believe far and distant shore.

Gerard A. Geiger, 1964

Trees

In my yard there is a tree
And also as far as the eye can see.
They grow all over this wondrous land
To shelter and provide for mortal man.

They grow tall and straight into the sky
And many people just pass them by.
No-one really knows how helpful they are,
The trees that grow near and far.

                                        Gerard A. Geiger, 1964

The Universe

The universe is a wonderful place
It is filled with stretches of unexplored space,
It has but not one bit of air
And with nothing else can it compare.
The universe is a blanket of endless sea
Where only God has the key.

Gerard A. Geiger, 1964

My Vessel

I have a little vessel,
Her sails' so white and trim,
That every time I sail her
I begin to grin.

She has a little steering wheel
That I can twist and turn,
And I always think that someday
I will sit at her stern.

And whenever comes that someday
I would be so brave and free,
But, alas, it is only a dream,
That truthfully, cannot be.

Gerard A. Geiger, 1965

The Inevitable

To live is to be happy;
to fulfill your desires.

To be just a man;
to master oneself.

By the torch of death,
your dreams set on fire

are quenched by the thought
of no more strife.

You have lived, lived in fear,
that you would expire;

you couldn't have known.

The cause of death,
which you have been dreading,

is life.

Gerard A. Geiger, 1970

Wandering

Like withered leaves floating on wisps of wind.
carrying with them days that now are past,
unknowing of their place of rest;
not caring of what was last.

So too, am I, a wanderer
searching for something unforeseen.
All knowledge and experience
will aid me in attaining my dream.

But many dreams are built on false hopes
my existence I may be squandering.
Yet if perseverance fulfills my destiny,
I will have given truth to my wandering.

Gerard A. Geiger, 1971

Earthlings

Crazy little beings
in such a rush down there;
with all the spoiled water,
and filthy humid air.

Always wanting things
which they have not;
yet never taking care
of all the things they've got.

Gerard A. Geiger, 1971

Whenever

Whenever I kissed your lips;
whenever I held you close;
you made me feel I was needed,
by you, who loved me most.

Whenever we walked together;
whenever we spoke our minds;
our love was real to us,
in those moments of time.

Whenever we clasped our hands;
whenever I looked into your eyes;
our love had not diminished,
it was not a fleeting sigh.

Whenever I'm dreaming of you;
whenever we're apart;
I know I will always love you,
and keep you close to my heart.

                              Gerard A. Geiger, 1972

Nature for the Civilized

Asphalt vines creeping across continents.
Rectangular rock structures strewn
about the countryside.
Molded metal ore floating on the oceans.
Masses of oil, wood, and metal gliding loftily
above the earth.
Innumerable amounts of stripped trees connected
by thin wire—like branches.
Rivers and lakes glistening in the morning sun,
reflecting an oily myriad of odd rainbow colors.
A mammal stepping on a flower
with a foot encased in animal skin.

Gerard A. Geiger, 1972

King

Movement and speech deliberate,
flowing with an easy grace.
Lithe form with chin held high.
Set of mouth and tear glazed eye.

Soft words, mellow as dew,
thoughtfully laid in patterns of prose.
Rich with the knowledge of ages past.
A timeless spirit in a human cast.

An approving nod, a softening of his eye,
seeking to encourage or give insight.
With wisdom much older than his years.
Falling disconsolately on deaf ears.

Gerard A. Geiger, 1973

Victory

Massive sets of horns
crash together in a field.
Leadership of the herd
lost to the one who yields.

Iron clad warriors,
both of whom are brawling,
in an arena designed especially
for the sound of multitudes squalling.

Countless numbers of small insects
spewing from respective mounds.
Black and red in opposition.
A moving patch on the ground.

Legions swarming together,
flashing their colors, black and red.
Lost in the fury of battle.
Forgetting their wounded and dead.

Winners bathed in glory

Minds swollen with self-pride.
Hearts heavy with mourning
for the wasted lives of those that died.

Gerard A. Geiger, 1973

A Prayer

Persevere in your quest;
the outcome unknown.
Live the life
in which you have shown,
that all that a man
can make himself be
is a gentle spirit
endowed with a mind that's free.

Search for the knowledge
to increase the thought
of man on this earth,
as to what life has wrought.

Do not fall from the setbacks
encountered with strife;
but live for the living
and help give them life.

                        Gerard A. Geiger, 1973

Analysis of a Daydreamer

Dark and dismal is the spirit within me;
while burning desire racks my mind
to overcome the feeling of loneliness
to which I have succumbed.
As an only pleasure
life continues in my dreams.
A swirling myriad of multicolored lights,
fantastic expeditions, expectations,and
placements.
In a world that does not exist,
but only for my peace of mind
and the continuance of my normalcy.

Gerard A. Geiger, 1974

The Purposeless Man

He who steals from another,
the man with deceit in his eyes.
Triumphant in cheating his brother.
His life, a series of lies.

Living every day in the present.
No pause for reason or thought.
Wishing he had what he hasn't.
Discouraged by what life has brought.

Like a log floating on the sea,
he has no purpose or direction;
and a meager existence his life will be,
if he doesn't pause for reflection.

Gerard A. Geiger, 1974

Nightlife

The cloak of night passes its dark
shroud over the town.

From the darkness intermingling lights
and sounds emerge.

The evening worshippers patrol the streets,
seeking and stopping at points of refuge.

Through a frost stained window
a young woman can be seen dancing.

A door opens and a cloud of scented air is whisked
away into the night.

Bodies, walking under streetlamps, suddenly appear
then retreat into the encompassing darkness.

Countless heartbeats flutter for
temporary expectations.

Voices share moments of
inconsequential conversation.

Minds swell with the golden drink,
poured into many glasses.

A word of hurt, thrown casually from the dark,
leaves a quiet throughout the town.

The star is low. The moon is a whisper.
The clouds are darkened watercolors.

Bright light cleanses the murky veil of a slender dawn.

The night is lost; as are its patrons.

Gerard A. Geiger, Feb 8, 1975

Changes

A momentary loss for a planned gain,
the longing for what was had.
Realization of the feeling of need,
the melancholy edge of sad.

Quickening beats of the heart,
while body functions are slowing down.
Sweating desire for the need to move;
a mind inversion, oblivious to sound.

No regrets, but a definite loss.
Time, again will make one feel.
Continuing with the inner drive,
searching for the meaning of real.

Gerard A. Geiger, Aug 75

Of Revelry and Reveille

Last night, spent in a stupor.
Unrealistic flashes of the mind.
Slanted thoughts of logic;
a naive happiness generated
from the physical liquid.

The morning of a September;
crisp, clear, awakening.
The need to move;
desire, goal, lust for life.
…reaching outward…

can you grasp the wind?

Gerard A. Geiger, Sept 75

Why?

The man moves through a sun covered sky,
seeking the answer before he will die.
Who has been before him, will be once again.
Another man thinks as they did then.

The man decides on a course to follow;
incorporating the past while searching tomorrow.
He takes his time to find his way.
The other is content to live for the day.

The man believes in the truth of one's mind;
blending his spirit with others his kind.
Sorting the knowledge gained through the ages.
The other stares blankly, accepting the pages.

The man has passed pulpits where other men stood.
He understands life, as any man could.
A trace of longing wets the corner of his eye;
for the other man has not asked the question,
"Why ?"

          Gerard A. Geiger, May 8, 1975

The Fisherman

A mild urge for pleasure;
the hook is fastened
and the line cast out.
The catch is mediocre,
but lonliness makes it suffice.

The business has been transacted;
a date the following Saturday.
Preparations, preparations-
Another fight with chastity;
1976 vs. the Puritan Ethic.

The night arrives-
The fish has changed her scales.
The show; a dinner; a cocktail-
The minnow looks with loving eyes.
Time to fish for trout.

                                      Gerard A. Geiger, 1976

Termination

Cancerous feelings of guilt,
enshrouded in a strangled mind,
makes one reach for the metal;
a projectile shattering mental bile.

The twisted form of flesh,
tattered, with a gaping hole;
the mechanisms damaged,
open to the air.

It grows cold in uselessness
as the wasted form such lies,
yet the mind is even colder
in he, whose emotions die.

Gerard A. Geiger, Nov 76

The Human Real

Sordid minds
with insecure thoughts
of sacred, but spoiled,
sacrificial tripe.

Emaciated immigrants
in disheveled clothes,
sleeping in sewers;
their lives floating down the drain,
through their urine crusted shorts.

Whores with flakes on vital organs,
gloating over twenty dollar bills;
as green as the scum on their souls.

Dirty metal cars piled with
grease and industrial smegma,
riding on rock—leveled roads;
wishing they could vomit
the living from the cushions within.

Pitying the virgin
for the evil thoughts of smut
which naturally invade her mind.

The tongue of a dog
lying on the side of the road;
swelling with the heat of the summer-
bloated with maggots.

The first puke;
a blob of green gerber's baby food,
staining a mother's blouse—love.

Slanted eyes raised to heaven
—ribs protruding from the chest
—metal on flesh
—hail to the victor!
—whomever he may be.

Rusted iron implements
from an age of other men
corroding like their makers,
as if they don't belong.

Festoons of logic
hanging from sculptured cement
etched on the walls of man,
the almighty lie
—the lie of universal truth.

Images of goodness
invading rational minds
—distorted behavior of animals
incarcerated within puritan ethic.

As the blood flows, the motor pumps-
the distributor and wires intact.
The mass moves, physically free;
subconscious desire is thrust like dead sailors
into the enveloping oceans of the mind.

Oh, emancipation!
A million years too late-
A million years too late.

Gerard A. Geiger, Feb 5, 1976

Rationalizing the Irrational

Sitting in my empty room
dreaming thoughts of you;
who was so close just moments ago,
yet now separated by an infinite distance.

Your lips; your eyes; your hair;
your smile; your laugh;
your look of wonder and awe;
are subject to the scrutiny
of an abstract and distorted memory.

Oh, the prejudice of time,
who but hours ago knew you as you are;
endeavors to erase your existence
from a mind already weary
with the longings of loneliness.

Your caresses, how real they were.
How remotely fresh their touch is felt.
The resilience of the skin bears
no recognition of your presence.

The love?
A desire not of the heart,
for that alone could not affect;
the singularity of the word
leaves an empty thought.

The striving of the mind
to cope; to comprehend;
to analyze and decipher
the meaning of desire.

The mending of the spirit,
as one with you,

now a mere shadow of
the structure of vitality.

Aggression? No.
Not towards things tangible.
Rather, towards the escape
and fleeting solidarity
of the bond of our existence.

The need, unsatisfied,
reappears to torment the vacant
space of tattered emotions
in which you had stood.

Hope for the realization
of a stable universe, is
lost in the contemplation
of the passing whims of fate.

Substitution, as a solution;
though prevalent, will only
sustain the loss
until a darker time…

The belief of the incapability
of assessing the relationship
between us, results from the
recognition of your absence
from the whole.

If this be love, then doomed I am.

Gerard A. Geiger, Nov 13, 1976

Thanksgiving 76

The river is young. For two and two tenths
decades the rich currents have flowed, washing the
threats from the citadel of the spirit.

Giving strength in surges,
weaknesses languishing
in-between, while silent contemplation
awaits a calm.

The rhythm is steady.
The pulse of life continues
in the swing of a pendulum, controlled
by the coercive emotions of the mind.

Agility of the appendages, maintenance of the
senses, and mechanisms of the mind intact;
give realization to the obstacles
encountered and overcome,
and further educates the being
in gratitude for his wholeness.

The processes of assimilation,
socialization, and progression;
attest to the aggressive nature of the
cognitive function. Both active and passive, relying
on the conditions of normalcy contained
in the recesses of unknown energies.
Emotions of thoughts. The luxury of exploring the
intangible is afforded only to he who has shelter from
the rude elements of nature.

Thankfulness and sincerity of progression are not virtues, but the logic of a rational mind which owes its existence to the methodology of its predecessors.

Gerard A. Geiger

Honour

The official charge had been given.
Over the fields the men were driven.
Fragments of metal, hurled through air,
smote them down and buried them there.

A red stream flowed across the plain.
Upon its banks the battle waned.
Discharging muskets, so often repeated,
barked with no mercy at the defeated.

At dusk the somber scene lay still.
The night cast down its dark death chill.
No warmth was found on that field.
The dead no longer push or yield.

Outlined by the moon a soldier stood
on a hill overlooking the field of blood.
The stars of night were gleaming brightly.
Those on his shoulders were tarnished slightly.

Shaking his head, with his arms opened wide,
trying to embrace those who had died.
Brave soldiers all, he had commanded;
now lay still with justice demanded.

Muttering a curse and heaving a sigh,
he grasped the pistol at his side.
Placing the muzzle against his head,
he repented; then left to join the dead.

Gerard A. Geiger, Dec 21, 1976

Indulgence

Flesh on flesh,
blending of body and mind.
Inner desire generating warmth.
Growing excitement of lust.

Arching upwards, muscles taut.
Looking through closed eyelids.
Finding a hidden point of light.
Succumbing to the physical and real.

Gerard A. Geiger

Crosswalk

Sunlight twinkling on a splash of silver,
replacing the spark of hooded eyes.

Tired feet plodding over the curb,
making their crude way to the center of pavement.

An old limb, supple still, raised towards moving metal.

Screeching brakes reply to an outstretched withered hand.

A lateral turn; the weary arm beckons
to a throng of children.

Raindrops of laughter sprinkle on the road with
the passing of brightly buckled shoes and sneakers.

The figure ambles to his station;
secure, as the guardian of the future.

Gerard A. Geiger, Feb 9, 1977

The Relationship

Exchanges of laughter bubbling
through shining eyes.
Flashing smiles lingering in
mutual admiration.
Nonchalant swaggers boasting casually
of expected intimacies.
Caresses of fragrance assailing hungry senses.
Passing time in the excitement
of growing emotions.
Touching the resiliently cool
texture of nervousness.

A kiss; the light darting wisp of breath
captured between lips.
Embracing the fitted warmth
of fluttering hearts.
Words carelessly abandoned
with the rising urgent need.
Nakedly exploring dissimilarities in mutual recklessness.
Culmination of oneness in the sweating
bond of sweet satisfaction
Exchanges of laughter bubbling
through searching eyes.

Gerard A. Geiger, Aug 6, 1977

On Living

Like a bird, beating his winged path
through gusty winds,
I travel on my journey through
life's course…
soaring, searching, gliding, diving, resting…
The capriciousness of momentum and direction
controlled by instinct as much as thought…
Living: breathing, eating, pulsing with wants
and needs…
All, subject to the careless abandon of
one who is master of his own world.
Restlessness, being the product
of lack of purpose;

like those flighty creatures,
I move from bush to bush…
Pausing from time to time…
Contemplating whether birds grow old.

Gerard A. Geiger, Halloween, 1977

On Security

Society mocks individual achievement;
forever prepared to attack the straw man.

Reality everpresent within a being,
the inner voice should scream "I can !"

Truths are self-evident to individuals.
Incorporated in groups they become trite.

Each must seek for his own meaning
far from the security of collective insight.

Search for truth in one's own being.
Far from the collective norms professed.

Add individual meaning to existence.
Let this be the answer to life's test.

>Gerard A. Geiger, Nov 10, 1977

Apathy

Apathy, the lazy bitch,
steals an active brain;
leaving thoughts to wander,
while attention begins to drain.

The predicament of the world,
faced with an opened eye;
curdled milk of thought
lets all feeling die.

The kiss of her lips
will rape your precious goal.
To her, your love inspired,
you will render up your soul.

Then you will begin to rest.
On other's deeds you'll lie.
And when you decide to live,
you'll find you've begun to die.

                        Gerard A. Geiger, 1978

Reinforcement

The way is rough,
the mind is sore;
you've had enough
in the human war.

You look for aid,
a friend is there;
the life you've made
is easier to bear.

Gerard A. Geiger, 1978 ?

On Love

Restlessness becoming more
predominant day to day.
Vast introspective areas of
emptiness convulse with yearning.
The immeasurable vacancy lusting for fulfillment.
As the natural processes
continue, the being is
enveloped with the separateness of the singular.
The spirit, controlled by instinct,
emotion, and thought; no longer functions
with the authority of wholeness.
A need has developed which

overpowers it's stability.
Realization of the physical,
compounds the mental
strain in searching for the love.
Requisitioned forces,
summed up from within,
pervade every aspect of the being.
Attesting that the void in life may be more
dangerous than life itself.

                        Gerard A. Geiger, March 19, 1978

Pleasant Forces

Looking through shaded lenses, the heat
penetrating through open pores.

Lungs devouring the stale freshness
of a spraying sea breeze.

Ears ringing from the cacophony
of the timeless surf.

Seagulls, those stringless marionettes, dancing,
floating; suspended on gusts of wind.

Laughter of little monarchs,
dripping wet, as they
watch their diminutive kingdoms
washed to sea.

A horn bellowing a protest against the vast and
barren expanse of water and sky.

I stand in awe gazing at the horizon,
where blue meets blue;
two lethargic giants slumbering on a summer day.

Gerard A. Geiger, June 20, 1978

The Gifts

The meeting: Apprehension stirs in
encountering a prospective mate.
Successive conversation yields a common
bond of intimate thought.
Ever enveloping closeness excites
the senses to share.
Words, emotions, fears are exchanged on a
rapidly building foundation.
Caresses and oneness complete the bond of
trust for the future.

The parting: The solemn pledge is made.
Two hearts destined for freedom,

promising everlasting fidelity.
Voluminous endearing phrases ricocheting
from separate sources.

Seasons passing in expressions of prose and gifts.
The past, never forgotten, slowly
sinking into the abyss of the future.
The return: The anticipated moment
of renewed affection.
An incredible void—compounded daily;
waiting patiently for fulfillment.
Remembering minute details of moments
of pleasures past.

The meeting: A curtain of
smiles and nervousness;
anticlimactic silences.
"I've found another."—"So have I."

Gerard A. Geiger, Sep 12, 1979.

A Moment of Time

You exist and plan to see what comes.
Possibilities exist for all things to happen.
Your input neither hurries nor slows progress.

A dent, you can make; a crippling blow, never.
What will occur, will occur.
What will not, will not.

You can only administer your own life.
Affecting the people and things that surround you.
Though, in time, they too will forget your passing.

Live then for yourself. Make your deeds shine.
If you must be but a speck in the universe,
why not be a speck of light?

A burst of energy, swift and straight,
covering your trail with illumination;
creating highlights as well as shadows.

A beaming brightness in contrast with
the dark, the dull, and the drab;
rapidly advancing in eternity.

                                        Gerard A. Geiger, May 9, 1984

Commencement

Seven pounds, more or less, sliding into life…
flailing, sputtering, sucking the first breath.
Crying with exultation, outrage, futility, or fear.
Throbbing chest and shaking appendages…
capturing the power of existence.
Comforted by the gentle and firm touch of a parent…
sharing the first experience.
Reposing under the spreading warmth of heated lamps.
Slumbering securely, enshrouded in soft covers…
the only armor of transition.
The being has settled, establishing a pace;
conserving energy for hurdles ahead.
A journey has ended and one has begun.

Gerard A. Geiger, June 22, 1984

Serendipity

Pockets jammed with baubles;
treasures to be cherished and saved.
Scuffs and scrapes on clothes and skin;
testaments to the elements braved.

Missing buttons and unlaced sneakers,
worn armor torn and tested,
stretched beyond their tensile limits;
begging to be sewn or rested.

Small pistons driving forward
bounding over brook or bush,
carrying mud, leaves and grasses
onward in their endless rush.

Giggles and gasps of new adventure;
under a rock; behind a tree;
in a puddle or on a hilltop;
searching for new things to see.

Oh, the wonder and excitement
that accompany the joy of youth,
meandering at whim and leisure
without care, nor doubt, of truth.

Journeys measured in moments,
from dawn to dusk confined,
in a day of fun and frolic;
a treasure to last all time.

Gerard A. Geiger, Spring 1984

Snowflake

Tendrils of ice fanning outward
from a crystalline core
of frozen water dust.

Lazily gliding downward
passing through a sea of air.

Unhampered in it's descent
by a million possibilities
for destruction.

Culminating it's graceful journey
by clinging to the cool

smooth surface of glass
in front of the curious
gaze of a child.

                        Gerard A. Geiger, Dec 26, 1984

My Woman

She is real. She exists.
She's the one I have missed.
She's alive and I feel
that I want her so.

She's my woman. She's my prayer.
She's my freedom from despair.
She's my life. She's my wife.
And I need her so.

She was a dream, now come true,
making troubles seem so few.
My whole life was on stop
till she made it go.

She's my lover. She's my friend.
The beginning and the end.
She's my life. She's my wife.
And I love her so.

She's a world of her own.
Makes a heart from a stone.
Gives a man all he needs
to believe and grow

She's my woman. She's my prayer.
She's my freedom from despair.
She's my life. She's my wife.
And I love her so.

Gerard A. Geiger, 1984

Tradition

Of tradition, it is assumed, our
ancestors had valid reasons for
establishing the requirements.

Through following tradition, it is assumed,
the valid reasons still exist and
have some degree of merit.

By blindly following tradition,
without forethought of the reasons
for it's existence, we become
slaves to the prejudice of the past;
and immediately create our own
myopia for the future.

Rational death of tradition
is the liberation of truth.

Gerard A. Geiger, 1985

Pauly the Penguin

Pauly, the penguin,
was down on his luck.
He had no money,
just his black tux.

He sat on the ice
and started to cry.
Because he couldn't find
his black bow-tie.

Gerard A. Geiger, Jan 3, 1985

Comfort

What comfort is derived from material things?

Is not comfort associated with things familiar?

Things that have lost their mystery of luster,
but find beauty in utility and shared experience.

What replacements can be found for a pipe,
hiking boots, jeans, and fall jacket?

—the coffee pot, whose product
has inspired conversation?

—a rock wall built stone by stone through
passing moments of reflection?

—a table, whose every nick and scratch boasts
proudly the hash marks of dutiful service?

—the floors and corners of a home, worn and bowed,
settled and unlevel—the garnishment of existence?

I am surrounded by things that
tell of shared experience,

It is from these remembrances that my
comfort is derived.

> Gerard A. Geiger, July 22, 1985

Santa's Gift

Through a window laced with frost
on a misty Christmas morn,
peered a bright-eyed little girl
at a sleigh upon her lawn.

Beside it stood a pudgy figure,
dressed in red with fringe of white,
talking gently to his reindeer
while he cinched their harness tight.

He paused to light his pipe
and shivered from the cold,
then packed his sack full of gifts
and jumped to the rooftop bold.

She could hear his footsteps
on the roof above her head,
as he climbed to the chimney
and dropped to the fireplace bed.

She crept softly to the stairs
to peek between the posts,
while Santa filled the stockings
and placed gifts throughout the house.

When he stopped by the heater,
to warm his ungloved hands,
she thought, "How cold he must be,
flying at night to distant lands".

She scampered to her closet
and grabbed a scarf of red and green;
returning to her staircase perch
without ever being seen.

She whispered down to Santa,
"For you, I have a gift!"
and dropped the scarf around his neck
before his head could lift.

Santa smiled up at her
and winked a twinkling eye.
"I will wear it when I travel",
he said, "Across the Christmas sky."

Then he turned to puff his pipe,
and muffling a sniffle,
scrambled up the fireplace
giving a sharp whistle.

Back in her bedroom,
she watched him jump to his sleigh
to resume his journey
before the break of day.
Then he cracked his magic whip
and wore a bright broad grin
as he flew past her window
with her scarf beneath his chin.

Gerard A. Geiger, Dec 12, 1985

The Pursuit of Happiness

Most fleet of foot
is happiness.

If pursued, rarely can
be caught.

For what is thought to matter,
really matters not.

Life, itself,
is happiness.

With all the sights,
the sounds, and tastes.

For the key to happiness
lies within the chase.

Gerard A. Geiger, 20 Mar 86

Bison (Ode to the American Buffalo)

A beast of burden it is not.
No yoke adorns its crown.
Majestic, and stoic of stature;
master of the open ground.

Lungs heave as bellows,
sending snorts of pleasure and pain
from the massive bearded head
on a thickly carpeted mane.

Forelegs draped with sinews,
to push or pull or run,
carrying the mighty torso
over plains from sun to sun.

Such nobles led great herds,
of millions were their number;

meant to last for time to come,
but not immune to plunder.

For what was ripe in beauty
and lordly in its bearing,
became not a source of food,
but rich robes for the wearing.

Quickly herds were slaughtered.
The meat rotted in the sun.
Few beasts were left remaining
when all was said and done.

What is left is the legacy
of the beast, strong and proud;
for it survived the fashion
and truth now is its shroud.

Gerard A. Geiger, April 2, 1986

Stolen Time

Oh, what succulent morsels
of infinite points in space;
those slender stolen moments
of time spent not in haste.

Time syphoned from reservoirs
of work left uncompleted.
Casting off the regimen
with a spirit undefeated.

Strolling through the ordinary.
Experiencing the season.
Having not an alibi,
nor searching for a reason.

The self-imposed utopia
that gives mind and body peace;
for a being caught in change,
bringing a welcome release.

> Gerard A. Geiger, April 11, 1986

What was it?

Screech
Crash
Tinkle
Tinkle
A blend of metal, glass and flesh;
the still life potpourri of cancelled
emotions, dreams and desires intermingled
with broken machinery.

Of the forces driving reality,
what compelled this scene's occurrence?

Was it fascination of speed?
An obligation for social festivity?
An hereditary irresponsibility?

An honest, or dishonest, mistake?
…or, perhaps, an escape?

Was it flawed engineering of:
the machine?
the road?
the man?
the life?
the world?
the time?
the place?

…What was it?…

Gerard A. Geiger, April 15, 1986

Cindy

A certain inexplicable quality,
as vague as it is specific,
drawing forces from empty spaces;
wherein within me dwell innate,
inert, mute, and indolent;
until touched tangentally by
the essence of her existence.

Suddenly becoming acute in
awareness of being and
purposeful in life, worth living.

The riddle of a being worth loving.

Gerard A. Geiger, April 24, 1986

The Source

I see her in your eyes
and in your laugh and smile.
The movements that you make
were copied as a child.

The expressions that you have,
are a clear indication
of the flattery you bestow
on the subject of imitation.

Subtle, it may be,
yet the bond is of steel.
You are what is she,
and it's through her you feel.

For everything you are
and all you will discover
have their point of origin
within your darling mother.

                        Gerard A. Geiger, May 8, 1986

Aching Back

A return
to the past,
like wearing
an old shoe,
at first is
deceptively comfortable.
But, after
very few steps,
acutely reawakens
the reasons
of abandonment.

Gerard A. Geiger, May 14, 1986

Christmas Remembered

He turned up his collar
and walked in the wind,
snow swirled around him
as he tucked in his chin.

Moving, bent and hurried,
gasping blasts of air,
he funneled all his effort
towards the apartment stairs.

Grabbing the iron railing
with a naked hand,
he shuddered a shiver
and up the stairs he ran.

He lifted the metal knocker
and pounded it to the wood.
Clutching his coat at his side,
on the frigid porch he stood.

A light glowed in the entrance;
the door was opened wide.
A blushing woman answered
with a child at her side.

He fumbled with his clothes
and slightly turned away,
then coughed a sob of anguish;
of sickness; pity; or dismay.

He did not say a word,
but pulled a doll from his coat;

and gave it to the child,
who hugged it against her throat.

"Merry Christmas", said the woman.
He nodded, cold and gray.
"Merry Christmas", called the child
as the man walked away.

                                        Gerard A. Geiger, December 12, 1986

Virus

Microscopic organisms
invading living tissues.

Parasitic squatters
camping in your body.

Having the sole purpose
of achieving growth.

Creating their structures;
emplacing pilings and bulwark;
laying footings and building walls.

Using your material
to wall you out.

A hostile concentric

community within you.

Rapidly building, feeding,
and multiplying.

Within an area illegally
annexed from its host.

> Gerard A. Geiger, Aug 4, 1987

Chameleon

Think for a moment:

—of a world with no time
—of rivers and sunsets
—of mountains and sky
—of towns and cities nestled on shores
—of large land masses teeming with people
—of nights running into days; dawns into dusks
—of energy restive to active, active to passive
—of birth and death
—of living, breathing, eating, sleeping
—of the many smiles and many tears
—of all the rest, somewhere intermixed,
as points of incongruity
—of having no measure of beginning or end

All is changing textures.

Gerard A. Geiger 29 June 1988

Cut and Run

You have touched me so
I can't understand
what has happened to
This arrogant man

you stepped into my world
and brought shadows to light
You attacked my dawn
and destroyed my night

a mercenary of the soul,
you vanquished my pride,
made my daily life droll
left me nowhere to hide

A Foe I couldn't beat
Was your open heart
However I planned retreat
it followed wherever I'd start.

Damn oh Damn, I'm just a Man
what have I really done
Am I doomed to understand
or am I doomed to cut and run?

Only I can assess these things
only I can choose….
Take the fruit your love brings
or cut and run…and lose.

Gerard A GeigerMarch 1995

Ecstasy

You are my ecstasy
you've become a part of me
in everything I do
I can't help thinking of you

all those other thoughts
that my loneliness brought
have now gone away
where I hope they'll stay

each day the dawn arrives
brings more joy to derive
from the love we share
with hearts as light as air.

Its so hard to describe
my feelings for you inside
you've given back my dreams
making life more than it seems.

I know now I can survive
and even be more alive
as long as you stay with me
for you are my ecstasy.

Gerard A. Geiger March 1995

"Mystery"

You are a mystery
I cannot fathom you:
What your love for me
can make me say and do!

Your love is one that inspires
without a need for reflection.
A love that often requires
that I dare new directions.

You are a source of hope
on this bitter sphere
your love expands my scope;
purges my world of fear.

You propel me to heights
with vistas far and clear
and as I peruse the sights
You brace me by standing near

How you understand the mind of man,
send my agonies to their infancy,
take a simple man and make him better than
…is just a Mystery!

Gerard A. Geiger March 1995

Whisper

Music roars at events we attend,
seas of sound engulf us without end.
Guests engage in their idle chatter,
conversation blends and doesn't matter.

Sound waves that ride the stormy seas
are silenced when you lean towards me
and Whisper that you love me one more time
Whisper that you love me: in love sublime.

No cannon thunders quite as loud
as a whisper from a lover proud.
Your whisper is an opera; a serenade,
singing of our love and plans we made.

Your breath is fresh upon my ear
when you whisper the love I hold so dear.
Please tell me then, soft and low,
tell me of the love I want to know.

Whisper of our dreams and our desire.
Whisper as we rage with loves pure fire.
Whisper that you'll always be the one,
who loves me till our loving days are done.

                                        Gerard A. Geiger 22 September 95

The Challenge

Seven noble explorers, seven intrepid souls,
selected by excellence to brave heaven's shoals.
Embodied with the human spirit and a nation's pride,
tasked to test the waters of the celestial tide.

Boldly they went forth to capture a nation's dream.
Commanding a rocket, progress riding on its beam.
Their effort was emblazoned on six billion minds that day,
all progress exacts tribute through lives littered along the way.

Their lives were precious jewels, polished and bright,
with dreams and desires that eclipsed the farthest sight.
Their noble deeds and daring, for all they left behind,
must serve as testament for emulation by mankind.

Their triumph was their excellence, their sacrifice to all;
to six billion fellow earthlings who, in rapture, watched them fall.
Their spirit is enduring and will pass from soul to soul,
through all future generations to whom their story will be told.

Gerard A. Geiger Jan 28, 1996

Written on the 10th anniversary of the Challenger Accident

Our Love: Young and New

You sparkled when I kissed you.
I beamed when you loved me too.
We planned a lifetime together,
when our love was young and new.

We smiled when we were together.
You laughed at things I would do.
We dreamed a life of sweet dreams
when our love was young and new.

Shamelessly, we explored each other.
We cared what each would feel.
Our touch was light and tender
as our love grew deep and real.

But the years, tears, and heartaches;
tender thoughts that have gone unsaid,
have raised a wall between us,
dividing the love of our bed.

I search for words to say this.
You still are my love and my life.
Our silence has come between us.
We no longer love as husband and wife.

Yet still I yearn to love you
with kisses tender and warm.
My heart aches to hold you,
to find shelter in each other's arms.

Please try to remember
all the things we planned to do.

Remember the love we nurtured
when our love was young and new.

Hold my hand and we'll go back.
We'll travel swift and true.
Help us recapture our first dreams
when our love was young and new.

Gerard A. Geiger February 23, 1996

Sentinel

The clarions had sounded,
reverberating through the land.
The call was made to muster
for every able-bodied man.

From the hills and valleys,
from each hamlet and town,
poured the country's champions;
young, still dressed in down.

All their adolescent dreams,
their wishes, loves, and more…
were offered with their honor
at the altar of war.

They accepted the mantle,
the yoke of the free;

the obligation to preserve
their country's liberty.

For this they fought the battles.
Some were wounded. Some died.
Each life was forever altered
by their refusal to hide.

To those silent sentinels,
the guardians of the night,
who insured our peaceful homes
and sheltered our children from fright.

We give our thanks and praise
for the sacrifice they bore,
and pledge always to remember
their gift of service in war.

                              Gerard A. Geiger March 23, 1996

The River

Swiftly, the currents of water flow,
gliding over all obstacles below,
it glistens and sparkles, reflecting light;
mimicking stars of jewelled winter nights…

The river is a mountain stream
riding on landscapes of my dreams;
churning through pits of emotion;
overflowing with its timeless devotion.

The River, a resource of the soul,
nurtures me and lets me grow.
As floods create fertile land,
the rivers' scope is deep and grand.

The River adds body to a parched man.
The River is the wellspring for what I am.
The River is the nutrient for love to grow.
You are my River, my lifeblood, my flow.

                                        Gerard A. Geiger February 4, 1997

Tell me (what you need)

I am young and proud
My heart is hard, but pure
I have cut you from the crowd
But now, I'm not too sure.
I'm not so sure I can love you
In the way to keep you near
To hold you and warm you
To drive away your fears.

Tell me what you need
And I will make it so
Cause love is so new to me
I don't really know
please tell me what you need
And I will make it so.

I'm good at mending things
-Broken tools, machines and toys;
At sporting games and other things
Admired by men and boys.
But when it comes to Romance
I don't know what to do.
I fell in love and took a chance
A chance I want to take with you.

Tell me what you need
And I will make it so
Cause love is so new to me
I don't really know
Please tell me what you need
And I will make it so.

A man has an obligation
To conform to a code
And he stakes his reputation

On the values he holds.
Love has it's own rules
No man can truly know:
It's simply caring and consoling
someone special and love grows.

Tell me what you need
And I will make it so
Cause love is so new to me
I don't really know
Please tell me what you need
And I will make it so.

I don't know how to love you,
how to reach your heart.
Please help me to save us..
To keep us from falling apart.
You are everything to me.

All I dreamed for has come true.
Now, that my heart surrendered,
please tell me what to do.

Tell me what you need
And I will make it so
Cause love is so new to me
I don't really know
Please tell me what you need
And I will make it so.

Gerard A. Geiger Feb 16, 1998

Dreams and Sand Castles

You wrapped up my letters
Tied them with a little string
Put them on your closet shelf
With all of your old things
I don't think you ever cared
I don't even think you tried
You wanted more than I could give.
Then something in you died.

You're all dreams and sand castles
Nothing but wishes and fluff
I gave you all my love
But that wasn't enough
I tried to be all you wanted me to be
But every brick I laid washed to the sea.

You packaged up our pictures
And put them in a cardboard box
You took apart our fixtures
And then you changed the locks
You didn't show emotion
Your face didn't move a crease
Not a tear of devotion
shed, for a love that ceased.

You're all dreams and sand castles
Nothing but wishes and fluff
I gave you all my love
But that wasn't enough
I tried to be all you wanted me to be
But every brick I laid washed to the sea.

You cancelled our phone line
And redirected the mail
You moved all our belongings

And filled hot water in a pail
Then you started scrubbing
Every floorboard and wall
Started scrubbing out our loving
And didn't stop till you got it all.

You're all dreams and sand castles
Nothing but wishes and fluff
I gave you all my love
But that wasn't enough
I tried to be all you wanted me to be
But every brick I laid washed to the sea.

And then after the cleaning
A bead of sweat or a tear
Dropped on the ruby necklace
I gave to remember our fifth year.
Quickly you wiped it away
And dried your milky brow

Then threw out my latest letter
And briefly flashed a scowl.

You're all dreams and sand castles
Nothing but wishes and fluff
I gave you all my love
But that wasn't enough
I tried to be all you wanted me to be
But every brick I laid washed to the sea.

I wonder what I could have done
to make you change so complete
I realized now that I had won
And your deceit turned to defeat.
You had never really loved me
You never really cared
You were only playing with sand castles
and dreams floating in the air.

Gerard A. Geiger, February 18, 1998

At Time's End

Every flavor is a rich dessert,
Every scent becomes perfume,
My chest tingles in my shirt
When you enter the room.
I feel a swell within me
That bursts my body and heart
Whenever you draw near me
You give my nerves a start

Have I known you before
At a distant time's end?
Did we make a pact
To return to life again?
And begin our love's next act
Where we fall in love again?

The special joy you bring me
The comfort that you hold
The peace I feel with you
Are wonders to behold.
I feel I've always known you
We must have met before..
Was it in some distant time?
On a misty sparkling shore?

Have I known you before
At a distant time's end?
Did we make a pact
To return to life again?
And begin our love's next act
Where we fall in love again?

There are so many things about you
I think I already know.

I have feelings when I'm with you
That lead to a safe place we can go.
There, I'm sure, we'll be lovers
So much more than just friends
Cause we've been to that place before
When we lived at time's end.

Have I known you before
At a distant time's end?
Did we make a pact
To return to life again?
And begin our love's next act
Where we fall in love again?

You know that you can feel it.
I can see it in your eyes.
You have that special knowing look
That can see through guile and lies.

You're nodding yes, you feel it too
You've reached that misty shore
Where we lived and loved at time's end
When we fell in love before

Where we fall in love once more

I have known you before
At a distant time's end.
There we made a pact
To return to life again.
And begin our love's next act
Where we fall in love again.

Gerard A. Geiger February 21, 1998

The Diary

We started with smiles and letters
Love, building and getting better.
Sharing beginnings and days' end.
Then I found her diary, returned from a friend.
Dear Diary written on the cover leaf
Warned me what was underneath.
I rushed in where the angels fear.
We're trained to doubt what we read and hear.

Dear Diary suggests something rare,
Of personal dreams: young and fair.
To wander in uninvited,
Tempts the loss of love confided.
What reason can there be
For me to peer unscrupulously?
What should it be, I ask of my soul?
Do rights of love win over rights to know?

I shouldn't have looked. I didn't dare.
Did I need to know if she cared?
Was curiosity my driving force?
Who knows what will be life's course?
Does reading words she carefully penned
Establish a breach of trust to mend?
Shouldn't those secrets be kept inside?
—Not left out somewhere to hide?

Dear Diary suggests something rare,
Of personal dreams: young and fair.
To wander in uninvited,
Tempts the loss of love confided.
What reason can there be
For me to peer unscrupulously?
What should it be, I ask of my soul?
Do rights of love win over rights to know?

Or do words, when carefully written down
Have an existence that begs to be found?
The author's intent seems very clear
Words may be found if kept near.
Or perhaps the right of privacy
Is established by hiding from piracy.
With arguments made for either case,
Who would know?—there'd be no trace!

Dear Diary suggests something rare,
Of personal dreams: young and fair.
To wander in uninvited,
Tempts the loss of love confided.
What reason can there be
For me to peer unscrupulously?
What should it be, I ask of my soul?
Do rights of love win over rights to know?

I take a breath; I must decide.
My name, if mentioned, would fill my pride.

The answer to all her wants and needs
Would be mine to know and heed.
Such a script would let me know all.
Yet, such an act would ensure my fall.
Discovering her is the key to my pleasure,
I returned it unread: my greatest treasure.

Dear Diary suggests something rare,
Of personal dreams: young and fair.
To wander in uninvited,
Tempts the loss of love confided.
No reason can there be
For me to peer unscrupulously.
What should it be, if I ask of my soul?
The rights of love will win over the rights to know.

Gerard A. Geiger March 4, 1998

The Devil You Now See

I was never an angel, if you knew me.
I gave out more grief than I received.
True, most of the trouble that surrounds me
Came from plans that I conceived.
But, I never meant to hurt you.
Didn't know your heart was in the way.
Wouldn't think that you could love me
I never thought you'd want to stay.

I've been thoughtless, rightly blamed,
and at other times ashamed.
But, I'll try to be a better man.
I hope you'll understand
that the devil you now see
Is much better than
The devil that I used to be.

There were times I kept my dignity.
At others, I crawled to save my skin.
I've been proud of fully half I've done
The other half wasn't much to win.
I never questioned why things are,
Till you came by my way.
I didn't project too far.
never had a reason, till today.

I've been thoughtless, rightly blamed,
and at other times ashamed.
But, I'll try to be a better man.
I hope you'll understand
that the devil you now see
Is much better than.
The devil that I used to be.

I've been in many scrapes along the road.
I've won and lost a goodly share.

I admit, sometimes I was the goad,
But most of them, I finished fair.
The reason for telling you this,
Is a reason I never had before.
You should know my past is a mess
Before we go on anymore.

I've been thoughtless, rightly blamed,
and at other times ashamed.
But, I'll try to be a better man.
I hope you'll understand
that the devil you now see
Is much better than.
The devil that I used to be.

You've got something that thrills me,
I'm not too jaded to say.
It's something I never had the chance

To catch, before I scared it away.
Although I'm not the best example
Of the purest sort of soul
I swear to you I'll never trample
The new trust that we control.

I've been thoughtless, rightly blamed,
and at other times ashamed.
But, I'll try to be a better man.
I hope you'll understand
that the devil you now see
Is much better than.
The devil that I used to be.

                                        Gerard A. Geiger March 6, 1998

Reflections

I see your careworn face
Staring through the glass,
The wrinkles at your eyes
Squeeze the light from the mask.

Gazing at your visage;
Calm, dignified, and secure.
I remember how you were
When you were young and pure.

The first time I saw you,
too young for my taste,
your skin was light and pink;
the blush of youth adorned your face.

You grew much too slow then;
were never too quick or strong.

In the rush of youthful discovery
You struggled to belong.

I would inspect you, then.
Mark your progress in my mind.
Wonder what the years would bring
When the growing was left behind.

Somewhere we fell out of touch,
I didn't know you were there.
I pursued life's varied ways
With more tenacity than care.

During those blocks of time,
When we didn't connect at all,
I never noticed growing older,
Enraptured with the latest call.

You've always waited patiently
Through years at hearth and home,
Now, the ten year old within me
Recognizes your reflection as my own.

As the cycle is nearly complete,
I remember little the work I've done.
But my memory is overflowing
With the friendships I've lost and won.

It seems my memory's most vague,
With little to recount or share,
During those periods of time
when I avoided your knowing stare.

Gerard A. Geiger, March 19, 1998

About the Author

Gerard Andrew Geiger, born December 27, 1953 in New Brunswick, New Jersey.

Gerard, of German Irish descent, is the fourth of nine children from a 1950's era Catholic family.

Gerard attended Catholic school through the fifth grade. At eleven years of age, In the sixth grade in 1964, Gerard began writing poetry.

After High School he joined the Air Force, became a Security Policeman, completed a tour in SE Asia in the early 1970's, serving in Vietnam and Thailand and was discharged in 1975.

He completed a BA in Political Science and History from Rutgers College, Rutgers University in 1977 while working nights and weekends as a Bartender.

He performed a short stint as a traveling salesman prior to attending Graduate School at Fairleigh Dickinson University where he graduated in 1984 with a Masters of Public Administration (MPA).

For the Past 18 years he has been living in Port Murray, N.J. next to the historic Musconetcong River with his wife, Cindy, and their three children, Rachel, Hillary, and Shawn. Gerard has been employed as a Management Analyst in the Federal Government for the past 20 years. His hobbies are writing poetry, reading history, collecting 18th and 19th century pewter and colonial era artifacts and generally puttering around local antique shows with Cindy and their three children.

The complete Poetical Works includes 67 poems, written between 1964 and 1998, presented chronologically. Gerard feels all poetry should be enjoyed and interpreted in relation to the age and experiences of the author. This collection reflects Gerard's insights and concerns at various stages of his life, and Gerard welcomes all to review his thoughtful efforts.

9 780595 091874